The Making of Modern Law collection of legal archives constitutes a genuine revolution in historical legal research because it opens up a wealth of rare and previously inaccessible sources in legal, constitutional, administrative, political, cultural, intellectual, and social history. This unique collection consists of three extensive archives that provide insight into more than 300 years of American and British history. These collections include:

Legal Treatises, 1800-1926: over 20,000 legal treatises provide a comprehensive collection in legal history, business and economics, politics and government.

Trials, 1600-1926: nearly 10,000 titles reveal the drama of famous, infamous, and obscure courtroom cases in America and the British Empire across three centuries.

Primary Sources, 1620-1926: includes reports, statutes and regulations in American history, including early state codes, municipal ordinances, constitutional conventions and compilations, and law dictionaries.

These archives provide a unique research tool for tracking the development of our modern legal system and how it has affected our culture, government, business – nearly every aspect of our everyday life. For the first time, these high-quality digital scans of original works are available via print-on-demand, making them readily accessible to libraries, students, independent scholars, and readers of all ages.

The BiblioLife Network

This project was made possible in part by the BiblioLife Network (BLN), a project aimed at addressing some of the huge challenges facing book preservationists around the world. The BLN includes libraries, library networks, archives, subject matter experts, online communities and library service providers. We believe every book ever published should be available as a high-quality print reproduction; printed on-demand anywhere in the world. This insures the ongoing accessibility of the content and helps generate sustainable revenue for the libraries and organizations that work to preserve these important materials.

The following book is in the "public domain" and represents an authentic reproduction of the text as printed by the original publisher. While we have attempted to accurately maintain the integrity of the original work, there are sometimes problems with the original work or the micro-film from which the books were digitized. This can result in minor errors in reproduction. Possible imperfections include missing and blurred pages, poor pictures, markings and other reproduction issues beyond our control. Because this work is culturally important, we have made it available as part of our commitment to protecting, preserving, and promoting the world's literature.

GUIDE TO FOLD-OUTS MAPS and OVERSIZED IMAGES

The book you are reading was digitized from microfilm captured over the past thirty to forty years. Years after the creation of the original microfilm, the book was converted to digital files and made available in an online database.

In an online database, page images do not need to conform to the size restrictions found in a printed book. When converting these images back into a printed bound book, the page sizes are standardized in ways that maintain the detail of the original. For large images, such as fold-out maps, the original page image is split into two or more pages

Guidelines used to determine how to split the page image follows:

• Some images are split vertically; large images require vertical and horizontal splits.
• For horizontal splits, the content is split left to right.
• For vertical splits, the content is split from top to bottom.
• For both vertical and horizontal splits, the image is processed from top left to bottom right.

LORD PAGET'S

LETTERS AND TRIAL

IN THE AFFAIR OF

LADY CHARLOTTE WELLESLEY:

IN WHICH IS INCLUDED

THE ELOQUENT SPEECH OF MR. DALLAS.

———

TAKEN IN SHORT-HAND BY J. AND W. PLOMER.

———

LONDON

PRINTED FOR T. PURDAY AND SON,
NO. 1, PATERNOSTER-ROW;

BY B M'MILLAN, BOW STREET, COVENT GARDEN

1809.

[Price Two Shillings and Sixpence.]

THE
TRIAL
OF
LORD PAGET,
&c. &c

SHERIFFS' COURT, MAY 12, 1809.

THE Defendant in this case having suffered Judgment to go by Default, the inquiry to assess Damages came on this day, before the following

SPECIAL JURY :

MR COLLINS,	MR. STALTON,
MR. MORRIS,	MR WADDLL,
MR SUTTON,	MR COCKFRELI,
MR. STRATTON,	MR COLLINS,
MR HEMPS,	MR WARDLE
MR. HOOPER,	

MR. GARROW.

Gentlemen of the Jury,

This is a case in which Mr. Henry Wellesley, the Plaintiff, comes before you for

B

compensation in the worst possible of civil injuries Mr. Wellesley, Gentlemen, in the year 1802 became acquainted with Lady Charlotte Cadogan—the parties were both of nearly the same age; the match was in every way suitable; the friends on both sides approved the choice of the parties, and under these circumstances their union took place in September 1803. A match thus formed seemed most assuredly to promise happiness, if any thing human could be supposed to promise it. There was a parity of fortune, a sympathy of temper, and a perfect equality of rank— one of them was Daughter of an Earl, the other the Brother of a Marquis. There was no possible point on which either the world or themselves could accuse each other with having made an imprudent match. Under these circumstances, Gentlemen of the Jury, Mr. Wellesley had surely the best possible right to expect happiness; and if there was any thing certain and constant in human affairs, Mr. Wellesley might surely not only have expected it, but have been assured of it. And Mr.

Wellesley, Gentlemen of the Jury, would have been happy—as happy as any one would have anticipated from these circumstances, if every thing had been left to its natural course . but something unfortunately intervened to blast these hopes. In the midst of their domestic happiness, of their mutual content, and mutual love, Lady Charlotte, unfortunately for herself, became an object of love to another. She listened to his addresses, she became the victim to his seduction the snare was well set, and caught its victim ; the flatt r-ing fabric of happiness fell to the ground in one miserable heap of ruins.

Gentlemen of the Jury, I do really think, that I never was called upon in a more distressing case . it is my real opinion, and my true feeling, that I never had to present to you a case more full of the most distressing circumstances. It has been a custom, a kind of fashion, and I am really sorry for it, to call upon me to plead in causes of this nature, and this, therefore, is not the first time in which I have had the honour—a most unenviable honour on

the point of feeling—to address you.
Would to Heaven, Gentlemen of the Jury,
that I was less frequently called upon to
discharge this most unpleasant part of my
duty. I am known to many of you; and
I am sure you will do me the justice to give
me full credit, when I state that such are
my feelings. I should really be ashamed
of myself, and ashamed of my honourable
profession, if either myself, or any of my
learned brethren, could derive any satisfaction from being employed in cases of
this kind. The inconsiderable remunera-
tion, liberal as it may be in a pecuniary
kind of view, is no sufficient retribution
to a man of honourable feeling. It is
truly impossible, Gentlemen of the Jury,
to be conversant with so much misery,
with such a variety of real wretchedness,
without feeling a most painful sympathy.
I have no hesitation to say, that I frequently feel, and most painfully feel, for
the distresses of those whose cause I have
to advocate. I should not indeed be a man,
if I were devoid of such feelings.

But in all the cases of this kind, Gentlemen of the Jury, I never remember that any one has fallen to my lot, in which there were more unhappy circumstances— a greater plenitude of misery—than that to which I am now calling your attention I do most firmly believe, that in this wide town it would not be a very easy matter to select a case, which, in a suitable relation, would appear more melancholy than this. There is really nothing wanting, on the one side, to aggravate the guilt of the Defendant, and to crown, to fill up to its very brim, the misery of the Plaintiff. The Plaintiff has lost every thing, and the Defendant has taken it.

It is generally considered in all cases, to be the duty of an Advocate to act the part of a poetical describer—a rhetorical flourisher—to dress up his cause to the best possible advantage, to put it in the best possible point of view, and considering the peculiar end at which he aims, to sink all those parts, and those circumstances, which do not advance or which, on the other hand, might impede his progress Gentlemen of the Jury, there is no occasion for any of this art in the case which is now submitted to your attention. There is as little room as there is necessity for this operation of artificial advocacy. If it could be possible to put the hypothesis, that in a matter of this nature any one would wish for a case perfect in all its circumstances, he would surely wish just such another as the present. He could not possibly indeed require any circumstances which he would not find here.

But, to resume my narrative, Gentlemen, the parties, as I have said, lived in the most perfect happiness till the unhappy acquaintance with Lord Paget. It will appear in evidence, Gentlemen, that no happiness could have been more perfect than that of Mr. Wellesley and Lady Charlotte. It will be seen by the evidence of some of the most respectable characters in the kingdom, that a more exemplary pair did not exist in the fashionable world; that their affection was reciprocal; that Lady Charlotte loved her husband to the full as tenderly, and with as much honourable affection, and apparent constancy, as what characterized the conduct of her husband towards her Ladyship. To say all in a word, Gentlemen, there could not possibly have been a more perfect state of happiness than that which characterized the early part of the union of this since unfortunate couple. Is it not pitiable, Gentlemen of the Jury, is it not truly a subject for the most compassionate feelings, that such happiness should have a duration so short; that, in point of fact, it should have been scarcely complete, before it was blasted?

The consequences of the union of Mr. Wellesley and Lady Charlotte, was a family of four children. Yes, Gentlemen, this is a most horrible aggravation in this unhappy case, that Mr Wellesley, the Plaintiff, has four children; and that Lord Paget has eight children. Gentlemen, I anticipate, I understand, what must be your feelings on this melancholy communication. It aggravates this distressing case in more points of view than one. It has lately been proposed, indeed been adopted in the House of Lords, to enforce a Standing Order of that House, and hereafter to allow no Divorce Bill to pass that House unless containing a clause, by which the offending parties shall be prohibited from marrying with each other. It is not within my present purpose to take up your time with any discussion, or even opinion upon the policy and humanity of this regulation, but one effect it must certainly have,—it must certainly extend and perpetuate one of the mischiefs which constitute the evil of Adultery. The woman, once fallen, must remain fallen for ever. She must remain prostrate for ever. The means of restoration to honourable society are cut off from her. The family of whom she is a member, a daughter for example, can never hope to see their family honour repaired;—the mischief has been done, and the remedy is rendered impossible. I will not say more upon the subject. but, even supposing that this Order had not existed, the condition of Lady Charlotte Wellesley, the unhappy circumstances of this affair. would have been the same. It would have been equally impossible that these parties

should ever be united. It would have been
equally impossible that Lord Paget could
ever have given, or that Lady C. Wellesley could ever have received, any remedy
to their present complete degradation.
There was no need of any law, of any
Standing Order, to prevent these parties
from ever being united together. They
are both married, are both the heads of
families. Lord Paget, as I have said, is
the father of eight children, and husband
to a most accomplished Lady. Lady Charlotte Wellesley, as I have said, has four
children, and has an husband, whose case
I am now representing to you. Under
these circumstances, whether the Standing
Order of the House was enforced or not,
is of no consequence to them. It promises
no alleviation of their misery. Lady C.
Wellesley—I do not wish to speak harshly
of the unfortunate—but whatever she is,
that she must remain. There is no hope
of her restoration. She has fallen from a
rank, a station in the world, which she can
never re-assume. This is another peculiar

c

feature of this case; and with such circumstances, Gentlemen of the Jury, am I not
fully warranted in saying, that a more distressing case was never presented before
any Court, and that, in all the variety of
my practice, a more unhappy one has never
fallen to my lot to be concerned in.

My Client, Mr. Henry Wellesley, as is
indeed very well known to all of you, was
employed in a very high situation under
Government,—he was Secretary of the
Treasury; an office which at all times, and
more particularly at the present, requires a
very great portion of the time of the gentleman who fills it. Mr Wellesley, therefore, Gentlemen, was almost continually
occupied in the discharge of his public
duties, and was necessarily from home and
at his office. These absences gave Lord
Paget an opportunity to visit Lady Charlotte, and by duly availing himself of
them, by pouring his soft tale into the
lady's ear, he eventually succeeded but too
effectually in seducing her into a perfect
oblivion of her honour, in making her

forget what she owed to her husband, and what she owed to her family—in making her a miserable, a ruined woman

In cases of this kind, it has often been set up as a topic of alleviation, that the infidelity of the husband had provoked that of the wife, and that the fail of the woman was rather imputable to this previous ill-conduct of the husband, than to the seductions of a third person. It is certainly not possible for me to anticipate the line of Defence which will be taken by my Learned Friend on the opposite side, but of this I am sure, that he will not, because he cannot, attempt a plea of this nature. No conduct could possibly have been more strict than that of Mr. Wellesley. I am persuaded that nothing of infidelity, no single act of even levity, can be laid to his charge. Upon this score, therefore, I shall make myself perfectly easy; I really deem it unnecessary to say a word more upon this point.

There is another topic of alleviation which is usually produced, where it can by any possibility be produced, in questions of this nature—a plea is endeavoured to be set up, that the husband neglected that due care which the law requires; that he has become the instrument, as it were, of his own misfortune, and that he has no right to come to the law for redress, where an ordinary portion of prudence and discretion would have prevented the actual occurrence of the injury.

I am sure, Gentlemen of the Jury, that nothing of this kind can be produced as a plea of alleviation upon this subject, for well assured am I, that whatever attention could be required by a wife from the most affectionate husband, was experienced by Lady Charlotte from Mr Wellesley; he knew the value of such a wife as at one time she was to him, and knowing this he guarded her with proportionate care. It is true, Gentlemen, that being in an official situation, and having certain public duties to perform, and those, as I have said, most laborious duties, it is true, I say, that in such a situation he could not always be at home, he not could always be where his inclination and anxious affection would have led him to be—by the side of his wife. But, good Heavens, Gentlemen, in what kind of world must we live, if a man going out on his necessary business, cannot safely and innocently trust his wife at home. I do believe that the world is bad enough in all conscience, but I do not believe it to be so bad as this. Mr. Wellesley was in every respect a more than ordinary careful husband, and I will defy any one to shew, or even to assert, that in any one single instance he has forgotten his duty.

Thus, therefore, the matter stands as to the usual topics of alleviation. No one can pretend any charge of any nature against my Client. His life, as to conjugal duties, has been pure and unsullied; he has been guilty of no infidelity, he can be accused of no negligence, he has suffered a rapine, not a loss, the society, the virtue of his wife has been forcibly plundered from him.

In running over in my own mind every ordinary topic, and every extraordinary one, I am really at a loss to find any one which can be urged in extenuation of my

Lord Paget's criminality. I know the ingenuity, the eloquence, of my Learned
Friend; it has often delighted you, it has
often delighted me, but powerful as it is,
and prompt as it would be to supply him
with every thing possible to be urged, I am
persuaded that this cause is so naturally
barren of all such possible points of alleviation, that I am sure that even the ingenuity of my Learned Friend will be confounded. He cannot, I think, but founder
in the attempt. He will do all that is possible to be done, but his efforts will be necessarily confined by the natural impossibi-
lities of the subject. He will do all that so
much learning, united to so much eloquence, and so much ingenuity, can do;
but even so much learning, united to so
much eloquence, and so much ingenuity,
must sink beneath the disadvantages of a
cause like this. He cannot, I am sure,
make any thing of it. Will it be pretend-
ed, that the honour and virtue of Lord
Paget was overcome by that superior blaze
of beauty which encircled the head of Lady
Charlotte? will it be urged, that his fortu-

tude sunk unmanned and like a broken reed before such powerful beauty?

Gentlemen of the Jury, Lord Paget is of an age at which the judgment ought to have been mature enough to have withstood all such temptation. Lord Paget is of an age at which the reason ought to be enabled to hold a good rein on the passions, and to check, at least, that licentious violence, that atrocious ebullition of them, which destroy wherever they reach. Lord Paget, moreover, is a married man, has a wife and eight children. surely these are not circumstances which allow of such an argument as the one I have here supposed. The long habits of domestic life the natural influence of family-feelings, should, at least, according to the common course of nature, have softened down this licentious ardour, and certainly in a case of this kind, no allowance must be made for such excessive sensibility, as if it constituted a natural and invincible passion. From a contemplation of human infirmity, certain allowances are always to be made for the invincible violence of passion, but to be entitled to these allowances, to have any claim to these lenient considerations, the passions must be natural, such as men usually feel, and such as general and ordinary reason finds it difficult to overcome.

I am most strictly forbidden to say any thing which in the most remote manner can hurt the feelings of Lady Charlotte. I most truly feel for her most deplorable situation, and it would have been unnecessary to have given me any such caution. I do not believe that a more miserable woman than Lady Charlotte now exists; so extensive and so fatal has been the mischief which this unhappy affair has produced. But whilst I entertain such feelings for Lady Charlotte, I must do justice to my Client. I must boldly proclaim, because I can truly proclaim, that a more miserable incident than this has never occurred; that on the part of Mr. Wellesley it was wholly unprovoked, and is without any possible alleviation or extenuation to be found from any thing in his conduct. Of all the cases which are daily presented to you, I know not one which has been so purely without any possible circumstance of diminution. It will be given in Evidence, that no life could be possibly more happy than that of Lady Charlotte and her husband, previously to this unhappy affair. In the intervals of business, Lady Charlotte was always the sole point to which the attentions and affections of Mr. Wellesley resorted. And it will appear by the same Evidence, that Lady Charlotte, justly sensible of the value of such an affection from such a man, returned it with equal fondness. How melancholy a reflection, that a state of this kind of felicity, almost supreme, should have been thus interrupted by the interposition of an Adulterer. Had it not been for this unhappy occurrence, Mr. Wellesley might, at this moment, have been the happiest of mankind, instead of being the most to be pitied; instead of being in a state of distress so deplorable, that the lowest wretch upon the face of the earth, cannot regard him with any thing like invidious emotion.

Gentlemen of the Jury, I conceive it almost unnecessary to say thing more upon this point. It is unhappily one of those cases which speak too plainly for themselves. The circumstances are as notorious as they are evidently and manifestly miserable. There are cases, in which the consequent misery attendant upon misfortunes of this nature, may be very complete, may be very full, and yet this misery, though really great, may not be so visible, so intelligible, to the eyes and understanding of those who are not immediately near the parties. Such, however, cannot be the nature of the case to which I am now calling your attention. The circumstances of misery are here palpable, substantial, visible to every eye, however blunt, and intelligible to every capacity, however limited. The circumstance of a man being deserted by his wife—the mother of four children; himself therefore having lost his wife, and his children their mother—these are circumstances which must speak very forcibly to every one present.

On the other side of the question, the case is equally miserable, and equally intelligible. There is the circumstance of a wife deserted with eight children. Such were the immediate, the necessary effects of the crime of the Defendant.—Two families ruined—twelve children deprived of their parents—a husband rendered miserable—and a wife the most desolate and deplorable of any human creature. The situation of Mr. H. Wellesley is only paralleled by that of Lady Paget.

Gentlemen of the Jury, I am persuaded that I have said enough to you to put this matter in its strongest possible point of view; what I mean by its strongest, is in its natural point of view. A case of this kind requires nothing but a very simple exposition; all eloquence is misplaced when Nature speaks herself; it would be an implied charge against your natural feelings, and against your common sense, to deem it necessary to go more largely into this subject. The business, the facts, the circumstances, lie in a nutshell, and as I have before said, these facts are all of a nature which speak for themselves. Under these circumstances, therefore, I shall detain you no longer than will be necessary to prove such circumstances of my case, as in point of law, but from form rather than from any substantial necessit , are required to be proved. The marriage is admitted, the unfortunate miserable criminality is likewise admitted , because, unfortunately, it is too notorious to be denied.

Lord Paget is at this very moment living in adulterous intercourse, continued as commenced, with Lady Charlotte Nothing, therefore, is necessary to be proved, but that previous to this unhappy business the parties lived in that state of comfort and happiness, which the Law requires in order to justify large damages in actions of this nature. To prove that they did live in this happy state, I shall call the Dean of Windsor, Lord George Seymour, and Mr. Sydenham. With such Evidence as this to produce, I shall conceive it needless to call the domestics of the family ; but lest my Learned Brother should not be satisfied, I have them at hand, and if required, will call them.

I have now a few words more to add, in which I am personally concerned. It will be necessary for me, Gentlemen, to take my leave of you before this case is conclud-ed. I am sure you will have too much goodness, and too much justice, to impute this to any want of respect to you, or to the Gentleman who presides in this Court. The point of fact is, that the Court in which I am particularly concerned and en-gaged, is at this time sitting, and my at-tendance is almost instantly required. Hav-ing called my Evidence, therefore, I shall make my bow.

It would be an injustice to my cause, however, not to say a word or two by way of caution against what you have to expect from the Learned Counsel by whom you will be addressed in Defence. Gentlemen, you will be assailed by as eloquent an ha-rangue, as, perhaps, was ever pronounced in a Court of Justice. You must muster up all your reason, in order to enable you to withstand the seductions which the powerful oratory of that Learned Gentle-man will present to your imagination. But I have too much confidence in your justice, Gentlemen, to have any apprehensions that the cause of my Client will suffer by any such extraneous Defence; extraneous, I say, for what eloquence can do away the necessary result of the undenied and undeniable facts?

Gentlemen, having said so much, I shall leave my cause in your hands. I shall leave it to you to decide what is the suitable compensation for the injury which my Client has suffered. It is for you to decide, whether in this case there is not something of peculiar aggravation, some particular circumstances, which take it out of the description of the generality of these cases. It is for you, I say, to determine, whether such a seduction, effected by a married man, with so little temptation, is not of the worst possible species; and whether as such, it should not be visited with the most exemplary satisfaction to the party injured. The Law, avoiding any interposition in merely private morals, considers this species of seduction as a civil injury, and as in other civil injuries, gives an action on the case to the suffering party. As a civil injury, therefore, you are to consider it, and the measure of damages must be the measure of the injury. Whatever necessarily aggravates the injury, whatever adds to the degree of misery, or degradation, to the loss sustained, or to any circumstan ... husband, all these circumstances necessarily agg ... the extent of the injury, and must necessa y, therefore, be taken into consideration as forming the just basis of the Damages. It may be true, that a pecuniary compensation is but an ineffectual panacea, but it is the only one which is possible, and the Law, perhaps, or rather the practice of Juries, give it in greater liberality, because it is, even in its most liberal extent, so imperfect a compensation.

Gentlemen of the Jury, I am persuaded that under all these circumstances, it is perfectly needless for me to launch more largely into the case before you. It has unfortunately been my too frequent province to have to address you on cases of this kind. I am persuaded you will believe me when I say, that this is to me the most disagreeable part of my professional duty.

It is truly painful to me to be so conversant with human misery, and with human depravity.

Gentlemen, I must take my leave, and in perfect confidence of your dispassionate justice I leave my case and my Client to you. I see that my Learned Brother is already preparing that torrent of eloquence which, in ordinary cases might, and indeed must, sweep every thing before it; but I repeat, Gentlemen of the Jury, that this is a case, which as it wants no eloquence to dress it, so has it nothing to fear from any efforts to destroy or diminish its natural effect. Far be it from me, unnecessarily, to aggravate the feelings of those whom this affair has made wretched on both sides. I was instructed to abstain from all such topics, and as far as I understand myself, I have abstained from them. I must hope, however, that in so doing I have not left my cause obscure, I have not omitted any thing which might be necessary to do justice to my Client.

I shall now proceed to call my Evidence. I must premise, that more respectable Evidence cannot be produced in any Court of Justice. If the Court, however, after having heard them, shall think further Evidence necessary. I have it to produce. I can extend it to any length, and take up your time as long as they think fit to give it me.

EVIDENCE.

The Rev. Mr. Sloane sworn.

Examined by Mr. Garrow.

Counsel. Are you acquainted with the parties in this case, Sir ?

Witness. Yes, Sir, very intimately with Mr. Wellesley and Lady Charlotte.

Counsel. You are a relation, I believe, of the Family ?

Witness. Yes, a very near relation of Lady Charlotte.

Counsel. So that you were intimately acquainted with both of them ?

Witness. Yes, I have been long acquainted with Lady Charlotte; indeed ever since our earliest years. We were brought up together from children.

Counsel. Be so good as to state all that

you know respecting their manner of living together.

Witness. I can only say, that it appeared to me exactly the conduct which married people should observe towards each other. They seemed to me to be perfectly happy.

Counsel. And was this happiness reciprocal?

Witness. Most certainly. Both appeared to me to be very happy; as happy a couple as I have ever seen; there seemed nothing wanting on either side.

Counsel. And how far did your observation descend?

Witness. Within two days of her Ladyship's Elopement. Down to this period I never observed any thing but what argued a fond and mutual affection on both sides.

Counsel. Mr. Wellesley appeared as much attached to his Lady as her Ladyship to him?

Witness. Most certainly. They appeared not to have a wish or a thought beyond each other.

Counsel. So that you have no hesitation in saying, that down to the period of the Elopement, or very shortly previous to it,

Mr Wellesley and his Lady lived in the most perfect harmony?

Witness. Certainly, this is what I mean to say.

Counsel. Do you recollect, in all your frequency of visiting the family, any instance of the contrary? Did you ever see any thing which could induce a contrary opinion? Recollect yourself, and speak from yourself.

Witness. I cannot have any hesitation in saying, that during all my visits in the family, which from the circumstances I have stated were very frequent, at all times, and at all places; I cannot, I say, have any hesitation in declaring, that I never once saw any single instance of coldness, of indifference, or of want of affection.

Counsel. We are to understand this answer as comprehending Lady Charlotte as well as her husband?

Witness. I mean it to be applied to both. I remember frequently having to attend Lady Charlotte to the Play-house or the Opera, when we have both met at a party: Lady Charlotte would invariably drive home in the first instance to see if Mr. Wellesley was there, and if he were, she would remain with him, and not go. If he were at the House of Commons, she would go and meet him, and wait till the House was up. I saw nothing in all her conduct but what was highly proper, affectionate, and honourable.

Lord George Seymour sworn.

Examined by Mr. Garrow.

Counsel. Are you acquainted with the parties in this case?

Witness. Yes, very well acquainted with all of them.

Counsel. Did you visit in the family of Lady Charlotte Wellesley?

Witness. Yes, very frequently; Mr. Wellesley and myself were on the most intimate terms.

Counsel. Were you acquainted, and did you visit in the family previously to this unfortunate affair?

Witness. Yes, it is of this period that I am speaking.

Counsel. And how did they appear to you to live?

Witness. Exactly as became man and wife—a very affectionate couple.

Counsel. And was this affection reciprocal?

Witness. Yes, certainly; I speak at least according to my opinion.

Counsel. Then according to your opinion and observation, did they appear to you to be an affectionate couple; or what the world terms, an happy pair?

Witness. They always appeared to me to be so.

Counsel. You never saw any thing which could induce you to form a contrary opinion? I ask you according to your own personal observation.

Witness. I certainly never saw any thing which could have rendered it possible for me to form any other opinion. Both Lady Charlotte and Mr. Wellesley always appeared to me to be a most happy and affectionate couple. Each appeared to have the most suitable and proper affection for the other. Each seemed, as far as my observation went, equally affectionate, and till the moment of the unfortunate business, equally exemplary.

Counsel. And you can say all this of your own observation?

Witness. Most assuredly, Sir, I speak from myself, and from what I saw.

The Dean of Windsor sworn.

Examined by Mr. Garrow.

Counsel. Are you acquainted, Sir, with Mr. Henry and Lady Charlotte Wellesley?

Witness Intimately, Sir.

Counsel. Did your families visit previously to this unhappy business?

Witness. Yes, Sir, we were all on the most friendly footing.

Counsel. Has your acquaintance been of a long standing?

Witness. Yes, Sir, I was acquainted with Mr. Henry Wellesley very early.

Counsel. Then of course, Sir, you can speak as to the state of his domestic happiness; how Mr. Wellesley and Lady Charlotte lived together previously to this affair?

Witness. Certainly, my intimate acquaint-once with them gave me frequent opportunities of observing their domestic life.

Counsel. Then have the goodness, Sir, to speak according to your observation Relate what you observed, or your opinion upon it, that I may not appear to dictate to you.

Witness. According to the best of my observation, there could not possibly have been an happier couple; I never saw in any persons more decorous conduct. They both seemed most perfectly affectionate towards each other.

Counsel. And was this uniformly so, and on both sides ?

Witness. Yes, uniformly ; I never saw any thing otherwise.

Counsel. So that according to what you saw in your daily intercourse with the family, they were on both sides perfectly satisfied, affectionate, and happy ?

Witness. Such were my observations, and such are the result of them.

Mr. Sydenham sworn.

Examined by Mr. Garrow.

Counsel. Are you acquainted with Mr. Wellesley and Lady Charlotte Wellesley?

Witness. Yes, intimately.

Counsel. And has your acquaintance been accompanied with a family and frequent intercourse?

Witness. Most certainly, an almost daily intercourse.

Counsel. Has your friendship with Mr. Wellesley been of long standing?

Witness. Yes, I was well acquainted with him in India, and on my arrival in England I renewed my acquaintance, and visited very frequently in his family.

Counsel. Then of course you have had an ample opportunity of seeing in what manner they lived together, whether happy or the contrary?

Witness. Certainly, I could not otherwise than have seen.

Counsel. Have the goodness to state to the Court and Jury, not the particulars of your observations, but the opinion which resulted from them?

Witness. They appeared to me to be happy in the extreme; I never saw any couple whom I could deem more affectionate towards each other.

Mr. GARROW—Gentlemen of the Jury, my Case ends here, and I now leave it in your hands. I am persuaded that no one will impute it to any want of respect to this Court and Jury, that I now take my leave.

———

DEFENCE.

MR DALLAS.

Gentlemen of the Jury,

I never have had to address you on a more truly painful occasion. Well might the Learned and Eloquent Gentleman who has just left the Court observe, that in all his variety of practice, and surely no one's practice has been more extensive, a more afflicting case never fell to his lot. What he said upon this subject, Gentlemen of the Jury, was strictly true. It is indeed a most distressing case; it is one that humiliates me; it is one that, on due consideration, must humiliate me. Here, indeed, will be seen a most calamitous instance of human infirmity. I am persuaded, Gentlemen of the Jury, that no one will deem my unfortunate Client the most depraved of men; they will take his case rather as a sad example of human infirmity, which under an exposure to temptation, is but as stubble before fire. When they think of Lord Paget, when they recall to their minds all the miserable circumstances of the case, they will reflect upon our own general nature, and tremble for themselves.

Gentlemen of the Jury, the Learned Counsel who has left the Court, informed you of many points, upon which, with a humane consideration to the distress already in this case, he had been ordered not to touch. I likewise, Gentlemen, had one point of positive instruction—I was strictly prohibited from endeavouring to soften down any of the moral or religious evils of Lord Paget's conduct—I was strictly commanded to acknowledge every thing, and by the candour of the avowal, by the most free and open penitence to attempt to heal the wound, which is always given to morals by the bad example of the Great.

Under these instructions, the possible sphere of my Defence will be small indeed. I have not to soften down any of those dark shades of criminality with which it has pleased my Learned Brother to invest the act. No, Gentlemen, my instructions from Lord Paget are, to acknowledge that his crime cannot appear of a deeper dye to you than it does to himself; and that the earth does not hold on its surface a man more completely miserable than himself. If those who have suffered by him were of a nature, as I know they are not, to have any delight in revenge, they would find most ample gratification in the present misery of Lord Paget. Gentlemen of the Jury, Mr. Wellesley may be miserable, but let me inform you, at the same time, that Lord Paget is equally so.

As to the question of Damages, if it could have been possible for Lord Paget, in any way, to have anticipated the decision of the Jury, I am sure that he would most cheerfully have given as much or more as could be given by the most liberal construction of any existing Jury. It is impossible, however, that the Plaintiff can find any consolation in satisfaction of this kind; I think too highly of his nature to suppose for a moment, that any pecuniary compensation can heal his wounded feelings. The Damages, therefore, must not be highly rated upon this consideration. There are two or three topics, however, which have been so insisted upon by the Learned Counsel, that it becomes my duty to set you right. The question in point of Law, and as you have to consider it, is as a compensation for a civil injury, and you have no right to take into your consideration any quality which is not a component part of the case as a civil injury. The criminal features of this case do not apply, and must not be applied to it as a civil injury. The situation of Lord Paget, as a married man,

most certainly aggravates the immorality
of the act, as it applies personally to him,
but it does not aggravate the injury done to
Mr. Wellesley. Mr. Wellesley does not
suffer more from the injury having been
done to him by a married man, than he
would have suffered, had Lord Paget been
single This appendage, therefore, of
Lord Paget being a married man, and the
father of eight children, though it much
adds to the distress of the scene, though it
renders it afflicting and pitiable to a most
extreme degree; these circumstances, I
say, however melancholy in themselves, do
not in any way augment the extent and
compass of the civil injury; and, therefore, in the consideration of the Damages
which are to repair that injury, are not to
be taken into consideration. These circumstances may excite your pity, but as
Jurymen your pity must not mislead your
justice. You may feel as Christians, and
as moral men, but you are to determine on
Evidence, within the limits and compass
of your oaths, and not on your feelings

and sentiments. Gentlemen, I am persuaded you will not forget this.

It is true, that by Lord Paget's criminal
desertion, a family of eight children, and
an amiable wife, are reduced to the greatest
possible misery. This of course on the
part of Lord Paget aggravates the criminality. But in this case, you are not to
look to the criminality, to the mischief sustained by Mr. Wellesley and for that
mischief you are not to look in the family
of Lord Paget, but in the family of Mr.
Wellesley. It is necessary that you should
keep your attention fixed on this distinc-
tion; that you have the civil injury to compensate, and not the criminal act to punish;
that you are not here as the Vindicators of
Morality, as the Censors of Manners, but
as Assessors on the quantum of injury
sustained by one party, in order that you
may assess the quantum of satisfaction to
be paid by the other.

Gentlemen of the Jury, on which ever
side you regard this case, on that side must
you find it peculiarly distressing; and if

you view it as I do, you will find still more
to pity than to execrate. It is true, that
the families were bound as it were together
by the greatest possible intimacy. My
Learned Brother has mentioned this as an
aggravation of the crime; but it was this
very intimacy which, by presenting the parties with too strong a temptation, most unfortunately led to the crime. Lord Paget,
as I need not inform many who are here
present, is possessed of every accomplish-
ment which could fall to the lot of man,
and Lady Charlotte Wellesley had a sensibility, an unhappy susceptibility, which
rendered the society and converse of such
a man peculiarly impressive to her. In
plain words, Gentlemen of the Jury, the
parties saw each other, and loved each
other; the connexion began in friendship,
and terminated in love; in that fatal and
unhappy passion, which is the more dan-
gerous where it creeps on us unsuspected—
where it steals on our prudence, and as it
were pilfers us from ourselves. Lord
Paget was thus subdued by what has subdued the wisest and strongest of mankind,

—he fell before no common charms,—he was conquered in no ordinary battle.

Gentlemen of the Jury, if my Client had passively succumbed under a passion productive of such a compass of mischief, I should not have had a word to say. But instead of succumbing, Gentlemen, he fought as bravely against this unhappy passion as he fought in the first ranks of the Army in the discharge of his military duties. He struggled hard, very hard, to subdue the tempest within him. Lady Charlotte upon her part struggled likewise. Strange as it may appear, upon being connected with the circumstances which have of late occurred, Lady Charlotte was a religious woman; she had early imbibed a proper sense of religion. To her religion, therefore, she had recourse, but her recourse was vain.

> I waste the matin lamp in sighs for thee;
> Thy image steals between the Heavens and me;
> Thy voice I seem in every Hymn to hear,
> With every bead I drop too soft a tear

As to the Noble Lord, he upon his part, in order to get the better of his unhappy attachment, accepted a foreign command, and went abroad to fight the battles of his country. I need say nothing as to the manner in which he there distinguished himself. I need not say, that, impressed with the peculiar misery of his case, he threw himself into the midst of battle, and sought a relief at once from his passion and from his life.

In this he unfortunately failed—I must say unfortunately, for surely it would have been better for him that he had died in the field of battle, than that he had returned home, where he has achieved so much misery to himself and to others. Had he fallen in the field, his death would have been glorious, and would have been, perhaps, sanctified by public gratitude. His efforts, however, to lose his life were unavailing. Acknowledge, Gentlemen of the Jury, that in these efforts there was something which seems to entitle him rather to compassion than to execration. It was not in the power of this unfortunate man to forget Lady Charlotte whilst living, but he endeavoured to die, in order that he might avoid the crime.

Gentlemen of the Jury, I am persuaded that you will find there was something in this conduct which indicated the sensibility of a man of some honour, of some moral feeling. I am almost persuaded, I say, that under these impressions, you will deem my Client an object of your pity. I cannot avoid thinking, Gentlemen, that the contemplation of the case of Lord Paget presents a striking lesson to human reason. Who that had seen him the flower and pride of the English Army—shining in the first rank of the first soldiers in the world—looked up to with astonishment and veneration by both friend and foe—covered with military glory, and possessed of a rank and fortune amongst the highest of the country—who, I say, amongst those who saw him with all these appendages of happiness, but would have deemed him an object of envy?—Yet, in the midst of all these apparent blessings, Lord Paget was surely the most wretched of the miserable;

be had that within him, which converted all this good into so much weeds and stubble.—A Sun-beam struck him in his midday toil, and cut the strong man down.

Gentlemen of the Jury, I am persuaded that in a case attended with such melancholy circumstances, there is enough to speak forcibly to your feelings, and that it is unnecessary for me to press longer upon your time. I think that a very cursory consideration of this case will be sufficient to convince you, that there is more of misfortune, of the heaviest of all misfortunes, than of intentional wickedness, or natural depravity. But however you may think upon this point, I must again caution you, that you do not confound the criminality of the act with the civil injury. You must keep the wrong done perfectly distinct from the immorality of the act : you have to repair a breach, to mend, as far as money will do it, the broken fabric of domestic happiness; you have to compensate and not to punish ; to give damages of compensation, and not of penalty. I was most strictly instructed by those for whom I am engaged, not to start any subject, not to suggest any topic, which might alleviate your too severe consideration of this matter at the expence of a painful emotion to any of the parties concerned. I have endeavoured most strictly, as well from compliance with these instructions, as from the impulse of my own feelings, to keep within the chalked-out line Your judgement will very easily supply some topics on which I might have enlarged, and on which, in any other case, and on a similar occasion, I should have enlarged but the wishes of my Client, even though at his own expence, must be obeyed, and my Defence, therefore, must be necessarily narrowed.

Gentlemen of the Jury. I need not be told, that the practice of Juries has occasionally over-stept the strict letter of the Law, and that finding it difficult, perhaps impossible, totally to abstract their attention from the criminality of the act, they have confounded the injury and the crime in the same consideration, and have united punishment with compensation. To men like you, Gentlemen of the Jury, I need not insist, that this confusion cannot be justified—that its only excuse, and that a very bad one, is in the ignorance of the Jury. Those, therefore, cannot have the benefit of this excuse who are thus carefully put upon their guard against it. After what I have said, and what, if necessary, the Sheriff will repeat to you, as being a part of the Law of the Land, it will be unnecessary for me to insist farther, that in the consideration of your Damages, you should carefully exclude from your attention the question of criminality.

But, even in the point of view of punishment, if it were allowable to take it for a moment in this point of view, surely no one would wish to punish him severely, who is now in a condition of the most extreme misery to which any punishment could reduce him. Consider but a moment, Gentlemen, what was the former, and what is the present condition of Lord Paget;—but a few months ago, who would not have envied the condition of him, who seemed possessed of every thing which could render life desirable—whom admiration followed in his professional course, and whom every one anxiously wished to imitate, and none could hope to excell. Gentlemen, what a wide interval between what he was, and what he is; between his present and his former state.

When you take these things into your consideration, I am persuaded that you will not be of opinion, that my Client wants any severity of punishment to render him an example His present situation, as contrasted with the past, is a melancholy example—a most awful lesson, to all who have known or heard of him—to all who have known him in his former height of fortune, and who can contemplate him in his present prostration of misery. Let every one, hereafter, take a solemn warning from the example of this formerly happy, but now miserable man, how they admit the first seductions of vice.—Let every one learn this important lesson, that Temptation is only to be overcome by fly-

ing it in the beginning; that guilt is a pre-
cipice, and that every thing lies in the first
step.

Gentlemen of the Jury, I cannot expect
but that in this case you will give some
Damages against my Client. but from what
I have said. I must hope that you will not
suffer your passions to be worked upon by
any extraneous circumstances—that you
will not, as I have said, confound crime
and injury, and will not punish where you
have only to compensate. In all that I
have said, I have endeavoured most carefully to avoid any thing which might in-
jure the cause of morals. I have endeavoured most carefully to avoid every thing
which could so mitigate and soften down
the criminality of the case, as to detract
from the sentiment which it ought to excite
in the public at large. I have done this,
not only from my own feelings, but from
the instructions of my Client. He fully
feels what he has done; he is to the full as
miserable, as any one could wish him.

Gentlemen of the Jury, I will not press
longer upon your time. I will leave the

case as it is now before you. I would not
have said so much, but that it was necessary for me to undo some errors, into which
the arguments of the Learned Gentleman
who preceded me, and who has now left
the Court, might have led you   If I have
executed my task as I ought to have executed it, I have confined myself to this —
If I have done more, I have trespassed beyond the line which I had marked out for
myself, and which my Client had marked
out for me.   He did not wish me to be so
much his Advocate, as to be the organ of
his penitence.   I have only to repeat, that
he is in a state which every one must acknowledge to be truly pitiable.   He has
lost private friendship, and public esteem.
Even his former military renown is now
without effect   Every thing which he
formerly possessed is lost.   Immured in
obscurity, he must hereafter pass a life of
penitence.   He cannot venture into the
light of the Sun.   All these are circumstances which are not characteristic of that
obstinate, insensible guilt, which is the
proper object of exemplary punishment.

Punishment is not necessary to render him a public example, even if punishment could be justly awarded. But as I have repeatedly stated, it is not within your province to award any punishment. You are strictly and exclusively the Assessors of a civil injury.

Gentlemen of the Jury, this is all that I have to state, and I now leave my Client and my Case in the hands of your justice, tempered by your mercy.

CHARGE.

Mr. BURCHELL—Gentlemen of the Jury, it has been most justly stated to you that a more melancholy case than this was never presented before you. Both the Learned Gentlemen who have addressed you, have agreed in this particular, and for my own part, I am sorry that I must express my own concurrence.

The Evidence in this case lies within a very narrow compass. All that is necessary to prove is, that the parties lived happily together previously to this unfortunate

H

business, and the best Evidence has certainly been produced to prove this This Evidence was so short and so simple, that it becomes unnecessary for me to make any recapitulation of it; its substance moreover is undenied, and uncontested. You have to take it, therefore, as a proved point, that previously to this unhappy business, previously to this most afflicting seduction, the parties did live together as stated, that is to say, perfectly happy, and as became a married man and woman of the most exemplary morals and conduct.

Under these circumstances, Gentlemen of the Jury, I conceive it unnecessary to say any thing farther. The speeches of the Counsel were eloquent and able, but as they left the facts undenied, the matter stands before you in a form and shape which it is impossible for you not to understand. Gentlemen, you will be pleased to consider of your Verdict.

The Jury having deliberated, gave a verdict for the Plaintiff—

DAMAGES,

TWENTY THOUSAND POUNDS.

LETTERS BETWEEN COLONEL CADOGAN

AND

LORD PAGET

———————

When this unfortunate connection was publicly announced, Colonel Cadogan wrote to Lord Paget —

"*Cook's Hotel, Dover-street,*
March 23, 1809

"MY LORD,

"I hereby request you to name a time and place where I may meet you, to obtain satisfaction for the injury done myself and my whole family by your conduct to my Sister.

"I have to add, that the time must be as early as possible, and the place not in the immediate neighbourhood of London, as it is by concealment alone I am able to evade the Police

"H CADOGAN"

———————

LORD PAGET'S ANSWER

"*March* 30, 1809

"SIR,

"I have to acknowledge the receipt of your letter of the 28th inst   I have nothing to say in justification of my conduct towards your Sister, but that it has been produced by an attachment perfectly unconquerable.

"She has lost the world upon my account, and the only atonement I can make is to devote myself, not to her

H 2

happiness (which, with her feeling of mind, is, under the circumstances, impossible), but to endeavour, by every means in my power, to alleviate her suffering. I feel, therefore, that my life is hers, not my own. It distresses me beyond all description to refuse you that satisfaction which I am most ready to admit you have a right to demand, but, upon the most mature reflection, I have determined upon the propriety of this line of conduct.

"My cause is bad indeed, but my motive for acting thus is good, nor was I without hopes that you would have made allowances for this my very particular situation and thereby have largely added to the extreme kindness you have already shewn to your Sister upon this afflicting occasion —I have the Honour to be, Sir,

"Your obedient Servant,

"PAGET."

P. S. On referring to the date of your letter, it becomes necessary to assure you that I have only this moment received it.

COLONEL CADOGAN TO H. SLOANE, ESQ.
HIS INTENDED SECOND

"*London, April* 2, 1809.

"MY DEAR SIR,

"I have availed myself of the very first moment in my power to relieve you from the anxiety you have for some days past been feeling on my account, by assuring you that all communication between Lord Paget and myself has ceased.

"And in order that what has passed may not be misrepresented, I herewith inclose copies of the only letters that have been exchanged, and I have to request that you will shew them, together with this letter, to any of my friends, or of your own acquaintance, that might wish to read them

"When my Sister, after a separation of a very few days, returned to Lord Paget, and when I was convinced, by a variety of circumstances, that the fear of my resentment had no farther effect in deterring her from that connection, I could no longer restrain the impulse of my feelings, and immediately demanded that satisfaction from Lord Paget, which the laws of my country do not afford, but which I had a right to ask, and he was equally bound to give me, for the injury he had done myself and my whole family This satisfaction, however, Lord Paget thought proper to deny me, alleging, as his letter expressed it, "that his life is not his own, but my Sister's," and thus making the very injury for which I demanded satisfaction his excuse for not meeting me It is not unknown to you, that I have by concealment alone been able for some time to evade the Police, who, having anticipated the step I was likely to take, are still continuing in pursuit of me. Under these circumstances, it would ill become me to apply to the conduct of Lord Paget the expressions that my feelings at this moment dictate, and I shall therefore leave it to you and others to determine whether the line he has thought proper to adopt on this occasion, is or is not the most honourable

"I remain, my dear Sir,

"Yours most sincerely,

"W. CADOGAN

To H Sloane Esq

I

LADY CHARLOTTE WELLESLEY TO MR J. ARBUTHNOT

"It would be the height of ingratitude, were I not to try to convey my thanks to Henry Wellesley for his most kind and generous offer of taking home a wretch, who has so much injured him. I dare not write to him myself, but I implore it of you to say every thing which gratitude and feeling can suggest, to express my sense of the kindness of his conduct. His note was forwarded to me this morning, but, degraded and unprincipled as I must appear in the eyes of every body, believe me I am not lost to all sense of honour, which would forbid my returning to a husband I have quitted, to children I have abandoned. Indeed, indeed, my dear Mr Arbuthnot, if you knew all, you would pity more than blame me. Could you tell all the resistance that has been made to this criminal, most atrocious attachment, could you know what are my sufferings at this moment, you would feel for me. Henry has not deserved this of me. We have had some differences, and he may perhaps sometimes have been a little too harsh to me, but I can with truth assert, and I wish you to publish it to the world, that in essential, and indeed in trifling subjects, he has ever been kind to me to the greatest degree, nor has the person, who may be supposed to have attempted to lower him in my estimation, in order to gain my affections, ever spoken of him to me but in the highest terms of respect. About my dear, dear children, I must say one word. Do you think I dare hope, by any remote or indirect means, to hear sometimes of them? You know how much I love them, you are aware of their merits, and what I must feel at having quitted them, but I have the satisfaction, the inexpressible comfort of knowing they will be taken care of by their father, though their mother has abandoned them. My dear little Henry and Charles—Oh! God bless you!—I wrote every thing to my brother last night."

"*Tuesday Morning 7 o Clock*

"Since writing the inclosed, I have come to town, and if it is not repugnant to your feelings, I think I should like to have one interview with you, but not if you object to it any way. The bearer can bring you to me instantly, if you will see me; but if not, ask no questions."

———◆———

MR. HENRY WELLESLEY WROTE TO HER, IN REPLY TO THIS LETTER TO MR ARBUTHNOT—

"That, for the sake of her welfare, and that of her children, he would consent to receive her again, provided she would return and break off all correspondence or connexion with the person she was then with, but that she must return *instantly*, for the next day would be too late."

———◆———

It is not understood that Lady Charlotte Wellesley availed herself of this indulgence of forgiveness

THE END

Lord Paget's Letters and Trial in The Affair of Lady Charlotte Wellesley: in Which is Included The Eloquent Speech of Mr. Dallas

J. Plomer

Lord Paget's Letters and Trial in The Affair of Lady Charlotte Wellesley: in Which is Included The Eloquent Speech of Mr. Dallas
Lord Paget's Letters and Trial in the Affair of Lady Charlotte Wellesley - 1809
J. Plomer, W. Plomer
HAR05871
Monograph
Harvard Law School Library
London: Printed for T. Purday and Son, No. 1, Paternoster-Row; by B. M'Millan, Row Street, Covent Garden. 1809